Square Foot Gardening Guide

Grow Organic Fruits and Vegetables in Less Space

Simon Hamilton

Tusc. Co. Public Library
121 Fair Ave NW
New Phila., OH 44663

© **Copyright 2016 by Simon Hamilton - All rights reserved.**

This document is geared towards providing exact and reliable information in regards to the topic and issue covered. The publication is sold with the idea that the publisher is not required to render accounting, officially permitted, or otherwise, qualified services. If advice is necessary, legal or professional, a practiced individual in the profession should be ordered.

- From a Declaration of Principles which was accepted and approved equally by a Committee of the American Bar Association and a Committee of Publishers and Associations.

In no way is it legal to reproduce, duplicate, or transmit any part of this document in either electronic means or in printed format. Recording of this publication is strictly prohibited and any storage of this document is not allowed unless with written permission from the publisher. All rights reserved.

The information provided herein is stated to be truthful and consistent, in that any liability, in terms of inattention or otherwise, by any usage or abuse of any policies, processes, or directions contained within is the solitary and utter responsibility of the recipient reader. Under no circumstances will any legal responsibility or blame be held against the publisher for any reparation, damages, or monetary loss due to the information herein, either directly or indirectly.

Respective authors own all copyrights not held by the publisher.

The information herein is offered for informational purposes solely, and is universal as so. The presentation of the information is without contract or any type of guarantee assurance.

The trademarks that are used are without any consent, and the publication of the trademark is without permission or backing by the trademark owner. All trademarks and brands within this book are for clarifying purposes only and are the owned by the owners themselves, not affiliated with this document.

Table of Contents

Introduction 1

Chapter 1 - What is Square Foot Gardening? 3

Chapter 2 – How to Make the Process Organic? 5

Chapter 3 – Planning your Square Foot Garden 8

Chapter 4 – Building your Structures 12

Chapter 5 – Common Mistakes in Organic Square
                Foot Gardening 21

Chapter 6 – Composting Methods 24

Chapter 7 – Mixing your Soil for Organic Gardening 29

Chapter 8 – Guidelines on Choosing Plants 33

Chapter 9 – Planting Tasks 36

Chapter 10 – Growing, Maintenance and Harvesting Tasks 42

Conclusion 46

My Free Gift To You! 47

Introduction

I want to thank you and congratulate you for purchasing the book, *"Square Foot Gardening Guide: Grow Organic Fruits and Vegetables in Less Space"*.

This book contains proven steps and strategies on how to implement square foot gardening in your backyard.

Square foot gardening is one of the best garden maintenance systems for backyard gardeners. Traditional gardening requires a lot of effort in tilling the soil, dealing with weeds, watering the plants and other garden maintenance tasks. However, its results are not fit for the needs of backyard gardeners. If you use traditional gardening systems in your backyard, you will end up harvesting too many of the same type of fruits or vegetables at one time.

Square foot gardening requires some effort to set up, but it is easy to maintain. Because this system uses prepared soil, there is no need to dig up the soil in your backyard. This book prescribes using the later versions of the square foot gardening system. In the later versions, the planting boxes are above ground. This separates your crops from contamination present in the soil in your area.

Square foot gardening allows you to plan your harvest, so that you do not end up with too many fruits and vegetables at one time. You may plant only the specific amount that you need.

Simon Hamilton

Lastly, this book applies organic gardening principles in implementing the square foot gardening system. In this book, we prescribe the use only of materials and plants native to your area. For instance, some early sources of square foot gardening suggest the use of materials that, we have learned, are not sustainable. The researchers of this book looked into alternatives for these materials and included them in the book.

Square foot gardening is easy to implement and it is efficient in using space. Start your own square foot garden today.

Thanks again for purchasing this book, I hope you enjoy it!

Chapter 1 - What is Square Foot Gardening?

Square foot gardening is a gardening practice, which involves dividing the planting area into planting boxes. The ideal practice is to divide it into 4x4 feet squares. This gardening technique allows the gardener to use the space available efficiently. It also requires lesser amount of soil in comparison to regular gardening.

- The box sizes can be modified based on the space available to you.

Though we use the 4-square feet boxes in our example, you can adjust the size of your box according to the space available to you. If your area is narrow, for instance, you may create a 3 feet by 6 feet rectangular box.

- It requires less effort compared to traditional gardening.

By using this technique, you can plant a higher number of fruits and vegetables in your garden with minimal effort. In the past, people used to plant fruits and vegetables in lines similar to how farmers do it in fields. This method, however, is not efficient if you are only planting in your backyard. If you plant in lines, you will need to cut through your grass, so that you will have access to the soil under them. When maintaining your garden, you will also be required to spend hours removing weeds.

As you cultivate the soil, however, it becomes more conducive for the growth of weed seeds. When you water your planting lines, you also water areas where weeds may grow. If you are not used to working hard outdoors, you will realize that gardening requires you to spend more time catching up with the growth of weeds.

Square foot gardening uses special soil mixes that have no weed seeds. Because you are only watering a limited area, weeds will not grow in unused areas of your garden.

- You can control the amount of your harvest.

In traditional gardening systems, gardeners usually plant multiple seeds of the same plants in a seedbed. The ones that grow are usually transplanted to a column in the ground. In this system, all your plants grow at the same pace. You can also expect them to be ready for harvest at the same time. This creates an oversupply of certain fruits and vegetables at certain parts of the planting season. Most people are forced to preserve the excess harvest to save them from rotting.

The square foot gardening system ensures that you only plant the right amount of fruits and vegetables in your garden for your needs. We will learn how to calculate the right number of planting boxes in relation to your family's needs. In this system, you will not be forced to preserve excess harvest because you can control the number of plants that you can grow.

Square foot gardening is the perfect system to follow if you are someone who wants to plant fruits and vegetables in your backyard. It works efficiently when it comes to using space and it does not require a lot of work to maintain.

Chapter 2 – How to Make the Process Organic?

Before moving on to building your garden, let us first discuss how you can make you can make your square foot garden organic.

Defining organic gardening

If you are just gardening for your own consumption, you do not need to be meticulous in ensuring that your garden is organic. All you have to do is to avoid the use of pesticides and chemical fertilizers. Instead, you should use products that underwent organic processes.

Organic pest control

Instead of using insecticides, you can use organic oil designed to repel damaging insects. You can also use natural practices of removing and preventing the growth of pests in your backyard. The best method to use depends on the types of pests that you are dealing with. In most cases, you will need to manually remove insects, slugs, snails or worms. You can hand pick those that do not have toxins or allergens. You may also use sticks to scrape off scale insects that you cannot remove by handpicking.

You may also grow the pest's natural predator as pets, so that they will eat the pests. If your garden is infested with slugs, for instance, you may grow chickens to eat them. Chickens also eat other types of insects and snails. Limit their access to some types of plants though, because they may eat some of your harvest.

Lastly, you can use plants that attract beneficial insects and animals. Beneficial insects and animals are those that eat pests without harming your plants. You may grow leafy plants, for example, since these are the specific places where butterflies lay their eggs. Breeding butterflies will be attracted to your garden if it is composed of specific plants where they usually lay their eggs. Caterpillars are picky eaters and they will only eat the leaves of specific plants.

The presence of caterpillars in your garden will attract birds that eat them. These birds may also eat other types of insect larvae in your garden. This will significantly decrease the amount of worm pests in your garden.

Citrus plants are examples of plants that attract egg-laying butterflies. If you have some potted citrus plants around your garden, butterflies will lay their eggs there. In the process, they may pass by the flowers of your crops and pollinate them to promote fruit development.

Some backyard organic farmers go as far as raising native spiders and releasing them into their gardens to get rid of pests. These spiders used to control pest populations. Because we destroyed most of the spiders' natural habitats, however, populations of pest insects climb steadily. Reintroducing native spiders back into your garden will control the population of pest insects again.

Organic soil and fertilizers

Farmers and gardeners used to employ artificial means of cultivating their soil. Some used chemical substances to control the acidity of their soil. These fertilizers are meant to make the plants fat and produce healthier produce. In organic gardening, we do not use fertilizers that are directly absorbed by the plants.

Instead of feeding the plants directly, organic gardeners feed the soil with organic materials. The organisms in the soil break down these organic materials and the nutrients in these organic materials are returned to the soil. The plants then absorb the nutrients from the soil.

To make your garden organic, you need to use soil and compost native to your area. If the soil in your backyard is not ideal for gardening, you should buy soil from local gardening shops or create your own soil mix. Instructions on creating organic soil mixes are provided later in the book. Avoid buying processed soil because it is usually treated with chemicals to get rid of insect eggs and weed seeds.

If you plan to sell some of your produce and label them organic, you need to follow the criteria used by the government in determining organic crops.

Chapter 3 – Planning your Square Foot Garden

When planning your garden, you need to make a sketch of its top view. You can easily do this by measuring the dimensions of your garden and drawing a proportionate shape in a piece of paper. It does not need to be accurate. We will use the sketch to plot out where you will place your square boxes.

When choosing the areas in your yard where you will put your boxes, you need to find the spot with the best exposure to sunlight and proper elevation for drainage. You may also put some boxes in partly shaded areas if you are planning to grow plants that only require a few hours of sunlight.

Box size and number

After selecting the areas where you will put your planting boxes, you need to consider the number and size of boxes that you will build. The ideal box size for most beginners is 4x4 feet. A box of this size can be divided into 16 1x1 foot squares. You can put multiple plants in each of these 1-square foot divisions. If you are planting something that occupies more space, you can divide the planting surface of this box into 4 2-square foot areas. This will give bigger plants, like cabbages, more space for growth.

If your space will not allow you to build a 4x4 feet box, you may reduce its size to 3x3 feet. You may even shape it into a rectangle, instead of a square. When planning the size of the planting platform, consider the amount of space available and the convenience of maintaining it. Consider where you will put your path and how the water can reach all your boxes. If you are using a hose to water your plants, ensure that the hose can reach all your boxes.

Factors to consider when planning:

You need to consider several factors when determining the number of boxes to build.

- Space available in your backyard

One of these factors is the space you have available. For most people, the planting space will be limited. If you have a 20-square foot backyard lot, you can only create a maximum of four 4-square foot boxes in your space, if you take into consideration the space for paths and drainage. You need to plot your boxes on paper, so that you can make use of the space efficiently.

- Needs of your family

Also, consider your family's needs when deciding on the number of boxes build. In theory, a 4x4 feet box can grow enough plants to make a salad for one adult for each day of the planting season. Ideally, you should create a 4x4 feet box for each member of the family. However, if you like to produce more foods than needed, you may need to build 2-3 boxes per adult in the family, so that you will have an excess in your harvest.

Beginner Tips

If you are just about to start in square foot gardening, you may find it difficult to maintain 5-10 boxes. The workload of building the structure and maintaining your plants may overwhelm you.

As a beginner, make sure that the workload is sustainable. If you decide to make five boxes, for instance, you can start by building and maintaining just one box. As you gain experience in tending your crops, you need to decide if you still have more time and energy for more boxes.

You can increase the number of boxes per season. In your first season of using square foot gardening, for example, you can start with just 1 or 2 boxes. If you think you can still handle more boxes, you can add another one on the start of the next season.

Include the paths in the planning

One of the common mistakes that people make when starting their square foot garden is that they arrange their boxes too close to each other without considering where they will pass. The aisles of your garden are extremely important especially if you have many boxes. If the aisles are positioned properly, you can reach all your plants in all boxes.

To make sure that you have enough space for paths, align all your boxes when choosing their position. This way, your garden will look more organized and you can reach each planting box easily.

Also, consider the types of material that you want to use to cover your aisles. Without proper covering, your aisles will be dominated by weeds. If you do not use a material to cover your pathway, you will most likely spend a lot of time dealing with these weeds, instead of tending to your crops.

Start with the boxes nearest to the house first

It is also practical to position your boxes near the house. Ideally, they should be positioned in such a way that you can see all your boxes from your windows. This way, you do not need to go out to the yard just to check your crops.

Placing your planting boxes near the house will also make harvesting easier. For many types of vegetables, you will only pick the parts that you need when you need them. If your crops are near your house, you do not need to go far to pick the vegetable or fruit that you need.

Lastly, if there is wildlife around your area that may be interested in your produce, they will try to avoid your house at all costs because of the danger of getting caught. Placing your crops near your home will deter animals from coming close to them.

Consider shadows around your property

When planning the positions of your boxes, it is crucial to consider the shadows cast by the towering structures. Consider the amount of sunlight that an area receives. Most plants require 8-10 hours of sunlight a day. However, parts of the house that only get 6 hours of sunlight should also be reserved for shade-loving types of plants.

Drainage

Lastly, you need to consider the movement of water in your yard when choosing the best positions for your boxes. Ensure that you do not place the boxes in areas where water cannot escape. This is common in urban areas where there are only a few exit ways for water.

Before building your first box, observe the movement of water in your property when it rains. You may want to add soil in areas where water tends to collect and has no exit. If drainage is a problem in your yard, you may need to create a functioning drainage system before creating your first planting box.

Chapter 4 – Building your Structures

The raised boxes are the most used structures in square foot gardening. You can easily organize them, plus they are neat. These boxes make the system more efficient.

Why do you need to create boxes?

- They can keep your garden organized

When traditional gardens become successful, the plants tend to grow out of their designated lines. When this happens, most gardeners get confused on the initial arrangements of their garden.

By using the square foot gardening boxes, you will always know the initial design of your garden even when plants cover its entirety. You will always have an organized view of your garden.

- They serve as the first line of defense against pests

The boxes create a physical grid that defines the limits of your plant's growing space. If they begin to grow out of their designated space, then you need to trim or harvest them.

The square structures also protect your plants. Insects from the ground will not have direct access to your plants. They need to migrate upwards just to reach your produce. It will be more difficult for crawling pests, like slugs and snails, to reach your elevated fruits and vegetables. If path materials, like wood shavings or tiles, surround your boxes, the crawling slugs and snails will need to be exposed before they can reach your plants. This increases the likelihood of the natural predators seeing and eating them.

- Prevents soil contaminants from mixing with your soil mixture

If you live in an area with contaminated soil, the square foot gardening system will allow you to plant without worrying about the contaminants affecting your food. If you or the past owners of the property used herbicides, pesticides or other types of harmful chemicals in the area, chances are good that these chemicals are still present in the soil right now.

Many types of commercial pesticides and herbicides take a long time to decay. They are still absorbed by plants and are introduced to our bodies, decades after they were used. If you suspect that such chemicals are present in your soil, then use the square foot gardening system to grow fruits and vegetables in your backyard. You can build the raised boxes with plywood separating the soil mixture from the native soil. This will prevent the plants' roots from reaching the contaminated soil.

The boxes hold the soil you prepare and separate it from the rest of your garden soil. By using square foot gardening boxes, the nutrients of your soil will remain in a concentrated area. Your nutrient-rich soil will be fully utilized even by plants with short root systems.

If you put your compost directly to the ground as traditional gardeners do, then the nutrients created from the compost will spread into the ground and sometimes, feed the weeds that grow out of it. If this happens, your plants will be robbed of the precious nutrients from the soil.

Square foot gardening boxes allow limited weed growth. If you use weed seeds-free soil, then there will be no weeds in your boxes. If you use garden soil that has not been processed, some weeds may grow but you can easily pick them manually before their root system develops and use up all of the nutrients in the ground.

How to create the boxes?

To keep your square foot garden organic, you need to use untreated biodegradable materials in building your box. Most people in the past prefer to use synthetic materials for practical purposes. However, these materials do not easily decay when you are done with them.

Though natural wood does not last forever, it is a more sustainable material to use. If available, use wood with its bark still on. You can make the bark face the outer part of the box to protect it from burrowing insects and other types of pests that may damage the wood.

You can also use oil covering to improve the wood's resistance. Linseed oil, for example, serves as a covering to make exposed wood last longer.

Wood dimensions

You will need four pieces of wood for each box. When making a 4-square foot box, each piece of wood should be four feet long. They should be cut flat so that they can create a square when they are made to stand on their long side. They should be 6 inches wide and at least one-inch thick. You may use a 2-inch thick wood if a lot of people will be passing by your box. As the foot traffic in your garden increases, there is a high probability that the side of your walls will get damaged over time.

You can easily make a 4x4 feet planting box by using screws to attach the ends of the wooden planks. Allow the ends of the planks to overlap, so that you can screw them together.

To make the process more organized, you should rotate the corners. This system of attaching the plank also leads to sturdier walls. By rotating the corners, you also ensure that all sides of your box have equal lengths.

Use at least four screws in fastening the wooden planks to each other. This ensures that the attached ends of the planks are stable. If you use too few screws, the weight of the soil may push the planks, making them loose. Your box walls will fall when this happens.

Do your carpentry in a flat surface

One of the most common mistakes committed by square foot gardeners is that they build their boxes in the lawn where they plan to place these. If possible, do the carpentry in a hard and flat surface. Ensure that all sides are level as you screw them to each other. You can just transfer the finished product in its planned place, once you are one hundred percent sure that all the sides are parallel to each other and that the walls are stable.

Sources of materials

You can easily find materials for the walls of your box in lumberyards. If there are construction projects around your area, you can sometimes find scrap lumber lying around. Most supervisors will give you the wood if they no longer need it.

To complete your box garden, you will need a material, which will serve as the bottom of the box. The original square foot gardening guidelines suggest using tarpaulin scraps. If there are many unused tarpaulins lying around in your area that are about to go to the dumpsite, you may also use them.

If there is none, however, you need to use organic materials like plywood. Plywood is the best surface to use for the bottom of your box because it is biodegradable. If there are other materials lying around that will serve as a cover for your bottom, you may also use them to cut the costs. If you do not have spare plywood but you have more planks, you can line the bottom with these materials instead.

The purpose of the bottom is to contain your soil and your plant roots within the box. This will prevent your invasive plants from building root systems that they can use to multiply outside of the box. By creating a physical barrier in the bottom, you can also limit the movement of the nutrients in the soil. As you water your plants, some of the nutrients from the compost you added to the soil will be carried off by the water. These water-soluble nutrients may flow out of reach of some plants with short roots.

If you plan to grow certain plants with deep roots, you may choose not to add a plywood bottom to your box. Only do this if you are sure that the soil in your area is not contaminated with harmful chemicals.

If you choose to build a box without a plywood bottom, then you can use weed cloth to prevent the weed in the bottom from migrating upward. You may also use cardboard as an alternative to weed cloth. Remember to cut holes that will allow water to pass through the cardboard or the weed cloth.

If there are earthworms present in the soil in your area, then they will be attracted to the damp cardboard. They will eat the cardboard and multiply around it, creating nutrient-rich soil underneath your boxes.

Planting box assembly process:

1. Predrill holes at the ends of your planks

2. Position each one to make the box walls then screw them together. Make sure that the screws are in proper alignment with the plank. If they are not, the walls may become wobbly.

3. Position the bottom material (plywood) in box's place in your garden. Make sure that the material you use has holes to allow water to drain out of the box. If you are using a plywood bottom, then you should drill ¼-inch holes in it. You may place 2 holes per square foot to make sure that the water flows out. If the surface

where you put your box is tilted to one side, then you should anticipate where the water would flow and make more holes in its path.

4. Place the pre-prepared walls in a position, which allows them to surround the bottom material.

5. If you are satisfied with the position of the box, then you should start filling it with your prepared soil. Pour some water over it to make the soil settle to the bottom. When the soil compresses with the weight of the water, you will know if you need to add more soil.

Adding the grid lines

The gridlines of your box serve as the separator between plants. You can use any thin and flat types of wood to create these lines. You may also use string as temporary gridlines, but they will not last long.

In a 4x4 foot box, you will need 6 pieces of lath that are as equally long as the walls of the box. Here are the instructions on you to assemble them:

1. After filling the box with soil, you may now add the first layer of the grid lines. Take three lath pieces and place them on top of the box, parallel to one of the walls of the box. Set one foot space from each other. You can then use small nails or more screws to attach the end of the lath to the upper surface of the wall. After fastening the first three lath pieces in place, you will have three evenly placed lines crossing your box.

2. Do the same with the three remaining lath pieces but this time, you need to make sure that they are perpendicular to the first three. Once they are all nailed in place, the crisscrossing lath pieces should create 16 inner boxes in your 4x4-foot box.

3. Create holes in the parts of the lath pieces that overlap. Once done, place a nail or a screw in the hole to keep them in place.

You can use fewer lath pieces if you want to make bigger squares in your grid. After attaching the gridlines, you can now start planting inside them. You should position your plants in the middle of the square created by the gridlines. The squares created by the gridlines serve as markers on the space of the individual plants or group of plants. The root system and the leaves of the plants should be within the grid squares.

In square foot gardening, be aware of the size of each plant that you add to your box, so that you can allocate the right amount of space for it. You may plant carrots, for example, in a 1x1 square. You may need more space for bigger types of plants. If you add a bell pepper plant in your box, however, you may want to reserve around 2-4 1x1-foot boxes, so you can give it enough space to grow.

Building protective barriers for your plants

Because you are planting edible plants, you should expect them to attract certain types of pests. Some birds, for instance, may visit your garden and feast on overripe fruits and vegetables. If you have chickens or some type of herbivore pet, then you can prevent them from coming close to your fruits and vegetables.

A square foot garden is easier to protect than traditional garden arrangements because of its uniform size. If you plan to make a 4x4 feet box, you can easily protect it by making a 4x4x4-foot cage. However, you need to ensure that your plant is not taller than 3 ½ feet for this barrier to work.

You can use a chicken wire to make the cage and use wood as its frame. This kind of cage will be enough to defend your crops against birds and other animals that may be interested to feed your plants. Squirrels and raccoons may also become interested in the fruits and vegetables that you grow. Stray cats in your neighborhood or your dog may dig up the dirt when playing. The cage will protect your plants from all these threats.

Vine holders

If you are planting crawling plants, you may need a structure, which will hold the plant's growth up. If you do not put up a structure where the vine of these crawlers can hang on, they will wander off to other squares and eventually, crawl out of the box. Here are some instructions that will help you create such a structure:

1. Place 4 poles in the corners of the box. Burry the lower end in the soil to keep it upright. The poles should be taller than your crawling plants.

2. Tie each corner of the net on the standing poles. Ensure that the poles are strong enough to keep the net up.

3. When the first vines come out of your crawling plants, hang them on the net. They will eventually grab on the net with its roots and grow.

Growing plants vertically can be tricky. The key to growing plants that crawl upwards is to ensure that your net and support structures are strong enough to hold the fruits of the plants. Our pole and net structure can hold crawling plants with small fruits like beans. However, for heavier varieties like winter squash, you will need a stronger structure.

Instead of placing poles vertically upwards, you can position them in the shape of a triangular prism. You can use six poles for the sides of your triangle. Each pole should be partly buried in a diagonal position to the ground. The structure you are creating looks similar to a triangular tent. You will need two additional poles to keep your triangles upright and one more pole that will rest horizontally over the three triangles to connect them structurally.

Once the three triangular structures over your box are already stable, you can start tying your net structure over them. The net structure will guide the vines of your plants to crawl upwards to your stronger metal poles.

The stability of your structure will affect the quality of the fruits that will grow from your vines. The vines will not develop if the structure is not strong enough. They may crawl upwards but if the vines sense that the structure is slowly caving in over time, they will not grow thicker.

Only vines that grow thick will develop flowers and fruits. If your structure caves in, your vines will never develop fruits. Some vines may start to grow some fruits even if the structure barely holds its weight. However, even if the fruits develop, they will not grow big. Their growth will be limited by the amount of weight that your structure can hold. The stronger your structure is, the bigger your vines and its fruits will be.

Creating deeper squares

If you follow the instructions in making 4x4 boxes earlier in the chapter, you will have a box with soil only 6 inches deep. Soil this deep is enough for most small plants. Some types of plants, however, require deeper soil so that their root systems can fully develop.

For these types of plants, you can choose to create a 1-squarefoot box and place it over one of the smaller boxes of your 4-square foot box. You can use the same process of making this box as building its 4-square foot version. The only difference is that you do not have to cover the bottom. You can then, fill it with soil and plant your preferred plant over it.

For plants that require a wider area for its root system, you may choose to create a 2-square foot version of the box. This version will fit perfectly in the center of your 4-square foot box. If you place it in the center, you will have a square foot gardening pyramid.

Chapter 5 – Common Mistakes in Organic Square Foot Gardening

For most people, building a square foot garden requires trial and error. Learn from the common mistakes that people committed in the past, so that you will not repeat them as you make your own square foot garden.

Mistake 1: Digging up your yard

As mentioned in the box-building instructions, you do not need to do any digging with this system. You can plant directly over your lawn. You will need to use a material that will prevent the weeds and grass from crawling upwards. You will need a weed cloth to prevent this from happening. You may also use spare cardboard boxes for the same purpose if you are cost-conscious.

Mistake 2: Painting the inside of the box

Most people paint the wood to make their boxes more aesthetic and make the wood last longer. If you choose to paint yours, then make sure to leave the inner side of the wood unpainted. The chemicals in the paint may seep into your soil over time. The plants will absorb any chemical absorbed by the soil.

Mistake 3: Placing the boxes too close to the fence

When you put the boxes too close to the fence, you will not have enough space to crouch between the fence and the box. If you can only access the box on two or three sides, you will have a difficult time reaching some of your plants in the far end. Manual watering will also be more challenging than it ought to be.

Mistake 4: Not adding paths

Though efficiency in the use of space is important, never neglect the addition of paths in your planning. Paths allow you to have access to all of your plants without the need to stretch and risk hurting your back. They make all your gardening tasks easier. If you do not have access to some sides of your boxes, routine tasks like manual watering, trimming and harvesting will be difficult. Because you do not have a 360-degree view of your plants, you may miss some signs of diseases and pests in your ocular inspections.

Mistake 5: Not planning for the long term

When starting their first square foot gardening project, most people put too much focus on lowering the cost. Some of them skimp on the types of wood that they use. Low quality wood will only work in the short term. They will rot faster than their hardwood alternative.

Mistake 6: Not considering chemicals in store bought garden products

Because we are trying to keep our square foot garden one hundred percent organic, make sure to check all the materials that you use in your garden for harmful chemicals. Most store-sold compost, for example, are processed using herbicides. Read the labels of all the materials you use in your garden. If there are any indications that they prevent the growth of certain insects or weeds, then you can assume that they are processed with harmful chemicals.

Mistake 7: Not considering that the same plants from different sources may have different sizes

You need to be familiar with the variety of plants that you are about to include in your box. It is crucial to familiarize yourself regarding how fast they grow and how big they can become. Some aggressive types of plants can grow beyond the space you allocated for them. The more sensitive plants around them may have stunted growth because they hog all the space.

Mistake 8: Not automating the watering system

Watering is one of the most frequently done tasks when it comes to maintaining a garden. If you do not automate the watering process, then it will take up too much of your time. Your goal when setting up an automated watering system is to make sure that the boxes are watered regularly.

You should also make sure that water is used efficiently in these systems. A sprinkler system, for instance, is not that efficient in this kind of system because it waters, not only the boxes, but also the areas around it. As a result, it also promotes the growth of weeds outside your boxes. You need to find a system of watering your boxes that do not promote the growth of weeds to lessen the amount of work that you need to do.

Chapter 6 – Composting Methods

An organic garden should have its own composting system. You need to reserve space in your property where you can let wastes get recycled by nature. Your composting operation does not need to be expensive. You can even just pile your garden and kitchen waste in one side of the yard and allow them to decompose. If the available space is limited, however, then you may need to develop a space-efficient system designed for composting.

For organic waste to become compost, it needs certain ingredients from nature. First, it needs bacteria. You will find these bacteria everywhere, but they are most abundant in the soil. They are responsible in breaking down kitchen scraps and piles of leaves into compost that will make the soil richer.

Second, the bacteria will require access to oxygen. When you leave compost piles to decay without getting disturbed, the ones in the bottom may have no access to oxygen. In these parts of the pile, the aerobic bacteria will all die off because they cannot metabolize organic material without oxygen. The anaerobic bacterial will then take over. Large numbers of these types of bacteria in your compost can become harmful to your plants. You will know if your compost is decaying anaerobically if it begins to smell foul.

To prevent the anaerobic decomposition of your compost, you need to turn the leaves and other materials at least once every week. By mixing them up, the ones in the bottom will be exposed to air again, allowing the aerobic bacteria to do their jobs.

The third component is moisture. The beneficial bacteria will multiply faster with just the right amount of moisture. Too much moisture, on the other hand, will kill most of these bacteria. You may pour water in your compost once every 2 weeks, but you need to make sure that the water drains properly.

The fourth component is the optimum temperature. Because of the size of bacteria, they cannot easily escape when the environment becomes too hot or too cold. Freezing temperatures slow down the metabolism of bacteria and may even kill them. Extreme heat also kills them. Because of this, make sure that your composting areas are not too hot or too cold.

The decomposition process will generate its own heat. If you leave the bacteria alone, then they will generate the optimum temperature to speed up their reproduction and metabolism. Too much heat from sun, however, may kill the bacteria in the outer parts of your pile. To prevent this from happening, you should place your compost in a shaded area. If you turn them once every week, the inner parts will cool off, preventing the risk of overheating. The addition of moisture will also help regulate temperature, especially during hot days.

Types of composting set-ups

There are many types of methods in composting. You need to choose one that you can easily implement in your home.

1. Using a composting pit

The most common way of making compost is to dig up a pit and put all your waste materials in it. Brown materials like dried leaves and wood shavings should be at the bottom. The greener materials, like vegetable scraps and fresh garden cuttings, should make up the second layer. You should then cover the topmost layer with soil.

The depth of your pit will depend on the amount of materials you have. The more organic materials you have, the longer the decomposition process will take. After 4 to 6 months, the area should be ready for planting.

2. Using a composting bin

There are multiple methods that you can follow when using a composting bin. These refer to artificially made containers that will hold your organic materials while they decompose.

Using a composting bin allows you to control the contents of your compost. It may also allow you to use different methods to hasten the decomposition process. Some types of binds, for instance, are used for anaerobic decomposition. In this type of bin, the materials are allowed to decompose in a sealed environment. The lack of oxygen will make the environment more conducive for the anaerobic bacteria to multiply. This method of decomposition is generally faster. While regular decomposition may take 2 to 3 years, this method will turn organic waste into compost as fast as 6 months.

3. Trench composting

Trench composting is one of the most used composting methods among backyard gardeners. This method, however, works best only if you are using traditional gardening setups.

In this method, you dig trenches in your backyard 4 inches deep. You then line the bottom of your trenches with your organic waste. You should then cover them up with at least 2 feet of soil. Nature will do its job and allow these materials to decompose on their own. In just 2 months, you can start planting over the trenches.

4. Worm composting

Worm composting is gaining popularity among organic garden keepers. In this process, you use specific species of red worms and earthworms to hasten the decomposition process. In this process, you will need a vermicomposting bin. You can easily make one with plywood. The ideal size of the bin depends on the amount of organic materials that you want to turn into compost.

Using plywood and some scrap wood, you can make a box with 2 feet by 3 feet dimensions. Its walls should be 1 foot tall. You may want to add a stand to it to make it stand a foot or two higher from the ground. This will allow you to protect your worms from ants and other predators. You should then add holes at the bottom of the plywood box to allow moisture to drop downwards. Create two of these boxes and stack them on top of each other.

Fill the boxes with your organic materials. Worms are picky eaters. They will not eat certain types of organic materials. Most people think that they can feed pet droppings to worms. Avoid committing this mistake.

Worms are particularly attracted to paper wastes. Save up your paper and cardboard wastes for your worms, instead of throwing them in the trash. They are also interested in most types of vegetable scraps. The rule of thumb is to give worms sweet and neutral tasting fruits and vegetables leftovers. They will also eat fresh leaf cuttings from your garden as long as their odor is not too strong.

You should avoid giving them kitchen scraps from ingredients and spices with strong tastes like onion and garlic. You may give them leftovers of leaves from your salads. They also eat most fruit and vegetable peelings.

Worms are good at eating and multiplying. If you maintain the environment conducive for growth and reproduction, then they will keep working for you. However, if the environment can no longer sustain their needs, then they will try to migrate.

You can use this behavior to your advantage. When the first box is full of organic materials and worms, you should stack the second box on top of it. Ensure that the worms can easily reach the holes at the bottom of the second box so that they can transfer if they want to. You should then fill the top box with your next batch of organic materials.

Once the worms have consumed all the food that you have given them in the first box, they will move up to the box stacked on top of it to get more food. When the worms have all transferred to the second box, you can now harvest the compost they have created in the first one.

In the process, some liquid product will leak into the bottom of your bin. You should have a receiving container for this liquid. You can use this worm tea as organic liquid fertilizer. They contain a lot of nutrients and bacteria that will make the soil richer.

Hastening decomposition

You can hasten the decomposition process by cutting up all the organic materials into smaller pieces. Most plant-based organic materials have tough outer layers. These outer layers make them resistant to bacterial decomposition. Leaves, for example, need to dry up and break apart first before they can fully decompose. By cutting them up, you will give bacteria more surface area where the decomposition can start.

Chapter 7 – Mixing your Soil for Organic Gardening

If you follow the prescribed soil mix of most square foot gardening gurus, then you will find that most of the materials that they use are not sustainable. The soil prescribed in square foot gardening uses peat moss. Though it is a widely used water retention material in soil, it is not sustainable enough to use. Peat moss comes from decayed and dried sphagnum moss. They are common in bogs and conifer forests. Because of their commercial uses, large amounts of peat moss are harvested from these areas each year. At this rate, we will be using up most of the decayed and dried peat moss in bogs in less than a century.

Organic gardens should use sustainable renewable materials. Though peat moss is a superior soil conditioner, it is not considered as a renewable material. Peat moss was once common in the USA, just like it is common in Canada today. The conversion of wetlands into residential areas, however, has drastically decreased the supply of peat moss in most states. This is the reason why most of the peat moss used in the USA comes from Canada.

You can make your own soil mixture without the use of peat moss. Here are the ingredients for your basic soil mixture:

Garden Compost

If you plan to start planting in the next spring, then start composting now. Collect all the organic waste materials from your garden and let them undergo the composting process. Choose the composting method that you can do in your usable space.

If your first batch of compost will not be ready by the time you start planting, you may choose to use commercially prepared compost. As mentioned earlier in the book, however, you should make sure that it does not contain herbicides and other harmful chemicals.

Soil conditioner

As mentioned above, you need to find an alternative to peat moss as a soil conditioner. Peat moss and other soil conditioners do not add nutrients to the soil. They are excellent, however, in holding just the right amount of moisture for plant growth.

To make your garden organic, you need to find alternative materials for peat moss. Coir is one of the best alternatives and it is renewable and sustainable. In places with no access to peat moss, sawdust and rice husk are used as soil conditioners. They are both waste materials and you can obtain them at cheap prices.

Vermiculite alternative

Just like peat moss, we should also find alternatives to vermiculite. Books in square foot gardening suggest that a third of the soil should be made of vermiculite. This is a mineral mined in countries like China and Russia. It contains some minerals that plants need like potassium. However, because they are mined out of the earth, they are not a natural part of the ecosystem of most parts of the world.

Organic gardening requires that we use only materials that are native to our area. Otherwise, we will be introducing materials that may contribute to the destruction of the natural soil composition of our area. If vermiculite is not native to your area, you may use more compost in its place. As a result, you will need to use 2 parts compost and 1 part soil conditioner instead of equal parts of compost, soil conditioner and vermiculite. If vermiculite is native to your area, you may use it in your soil mixture.

If you use these mixtures in your square foot gardening boxes, you will be using a soil-free mixture. You no longer need to dig up soil for your gardening. If you prepared your compost with no soil, it will not contain weed seeds and insect eggs that may become pests.

You can also reuse the mixture every planting season. You will only need more soil mix when you want to add more boxes.

Mixing the soil

If you have decided on the proportions that you will use in your mixture, then you should start mixing them. First, you need to decide how much soil you will need. You need to get the volume of your box. You need to do a little math to know the exact amount:

Volume of the box in feet =

(Length of the box) x (Width of the box) x (Height of the box)

In this book, we used a 4 x 4 feet box in our examples. You can apply the formula to this size to know the volume of soil that you will need:

4 feet x 4 feet x 0.5 feet (6 inches) = 8 cubic feet

This means that you will need 8 cubic feet of soil to fill a box of this size.

Now that you are fully aware of the amount of soil that you need to mix, it is time to do the work. When mixing your soil mixture, you need to be careful not to waste any of the valuable soil materials. The square foot gardening community suggests the use of tarp. To keep the process organic, you should mix yours in a wheelbarrow instead. To do this, you need to put all the ingredients in a large wheelbarrow. You can then, use a shovel to mix the contents. To lessen dust in the air, moisten the soil mixture. Do not put too much water into the wheelbarrow because it will get too heavy and the mixture will be difficult to transfer into the box.

Simon Hamilton

Mixing in a wheelbarrow makes it easy for you to pour the mixture in your box. Pour the first half of the mixture into the box. Before adding the second half, ensure that the corners of the box are filled first. Once the first half is evenly distributed, you can now pour the second half in. Once you have transferred the mixture, make sure that the whole soil mixture is evenly distributed. The surface of the soil should be level.

Chapter 8 – Guidelines on Choosing Plants

Planting in a square foot garden is similar as in regular gardens. However, square foot gardeners are more efficient in the way they use their space. You can plant many types of plants in a 4x4-foot box. With just one box, you can plant all the plant components of a leafy salad dish.

Factors to consider when selecting your first plants

Weather patterns

In the previous chapters, we discussed how to make the square foot gardening boxes and the composition of the soil mix. Before you can start planting in your new boxes, you first need to know how long the planting season is in your area. In general, the planting season shortens as you move north of the equator.

Gardeners in Miami will have more planting days in comparison to gardeners in Alaska. You should be able to know how many months you have for planting through your knowledge of the weather patterns in your area. You should count the number of months between spring and the first days of winter.

In traditional gardening, the planting season starts when the soil becomes soft enough to till in spring. This happens when the weather starts to warm up and the ice starts to melt.

In square foot gardening, you can store your soil mixture to protect it from the coldness of winter. You can then start planting as the sun starts shining. If the weather starts to warm up, then you can start planting even when the ground is still too hard to till.

By knowing the number of gardening days in your area, you can plan the types of plants that you can grow with the time that you have.

Wind strength and amount of sunlight

You also need to consider the strength of the wind and the amount of sunshine that your area gets when choosing the types of plants to grow. Some types of plants cannot grow in windswept areas. You need to choose tough crops if you are located in a windy area.

Some types of plants also require a lot of sunlight to grow properly. There are some types of plants, however, that cannot grow if the heat of the sun is too strong. By taking the strength of the sun into consideration, you can choose the types of plants you can grow in spring, summer and fall.

Water source

Your choice of plants will also be affected by the amount of water that you have in your area. If your city has water problems, then you will have difficulty maintaining plants that require a lot of water. You should also take into consideration that almost all areas experience a dry spell from time to time. It is best to have other sources of water other than the water that runs through the pipes of your home. If there is a body of fresh water near your home, for instance, you should find ways to use it for your garden.

Choose native plants

When choosing the types of plants to include in your organic square foot garden, consider going for those that are native in your area. Look into plants that grow naturally in your country. These types of plants can surely live in your climate and they will be fit to deal with the wind gusts and amount of sunlight that your area receives.

Go to local gardening expos to find out what types of vegetables are being planted by other gardeners in your area. Also, look for local groups for organic gardening enthusiasts. Ask advice from the members of these groups regarding where to find the best organic seeds and gardening materials.

Plants that you use often in the kitchen

Lastly, consider planting types of crops that you often use in the kitchen. Commonly used vegetables should be included in your list. Some of these are potatoes, tomatoes and leafy greens. If your climate will permit it, you should also plant common root crops like beets and carrots.

Chapter 9 – Planting Tasks

When planting, you should start from seeds. To keep your garden organic, you need to make sure that you use certified organic seeds. Most seeds nowadays have already undergone some sort of genetic modification. To ensure that the plants you grow are organic, take your seeds only from sources that use only organic processes of growing and harvesting these seeds.

You can find seeds like these in plant certified organic farms and plant nurseries. If you do not have organic farms and nurseries in your area, you can order them online.

Planting seeds

To plant seeds, you first need to place them in a seedbed. Seedbeds are boxes where you allow the seeds to undergo the early parts of their development. Plants are fragile when they have just emerged from their seeds. Very small movements can disturb and stop their growth. They are also less resistant to pests during this stage. By planting them in a seedbed, you can put them in a secure location where they will receive controlled amounts of water and sunlight. This will ensure that your crops start their growth strong.

The number of seeds that you plant depends on the number of square foot gardening boxes you have available. You also need to consider the amount of work it takes to tend the crops. If you are a first time gardener, it is best to start small.

Keep the plants in the seedbed until they have grown strong enough to be transplanted to your boxes.

You can follow these instructions when planting in your seedbed for the first time:

1. Pick a suitable container for a seedbed

Any shallow container can serve as a seedbed. It should have a flat bottom so that the soil will be evenly distributed. Also, add holes to allow water to drain.

2. Fill it up with regular soil

You need to add regular soil to your seedbed. The soil is the medium where the seeds will break their dormancy. You may add compost materials to it to add nutrients. Seeds have evolved to remain dormant until environmental conditions are conducive for growth. Your seeds will not grow if your soil cannot hold water and has no nutrients that are prerequisite to the initial growth of the seeds.

3. Poke holes into the soil and plant the seeds

You should then add holes to the soil. Make sure that they are evenly distributed, so that each seed will have enough space to grow its root system. The plants are more likely to survive if other plants growing around them do not disturb them. You should then add the seeds in the hole and cover them up again. You may also draw a line in the dirt with your finger and line the seeds in small ditches you create. You can then cover the line of seeds and water them.

Knowing the exact number that you need to plant can be tricky. You cannot plant the exact number of seeds that you will use in your boxes because some of the seeds that you plant may be dead. Dead seeds will never develop regardless of what you do.

You need to use your experiences with the seeds that you are about to use to know the exact number that you need to plant. Let's say you are about to plant a full pack of lettuce seeds. The pack contains 50 seeds. Out of the 50, only 45 plants sprouted. In this case, only 90% of the seeds are healthy.

In the future, when planting the same seeds from the same source, you should take your past success rate into consideration when planning how many seeds to plant. Let's say you have space for nine leafy lettuce in your box. If the pack that you use has a consistent 100% success rate, then you may plant only nine seeds. However, because the brand that you are using has a 90% success rate, you should plant 10 seeds to get nine successful seedlings.

4. Water them regularly

You should water the seeds regularly. If you use good soil, it should be capable of retaining water for one day before completely drying up. Moisture is one of the primary needs of the seed for it to start growing.

You need to research the growth patterns of the plants that you are planting so that you will know when the first leaves should come out of their shell. Some seeds take just a few days before their first leaves come out. Others take a couple of weeks of watering before the first leaves emerge.

As you water the seeds, you may also activate some weed seeds left in the soil of your seedbed. Check your seedbed for weed growth at this point. These types of plants grow fast. If you let their roots grow, then these may affect the growth of your crops. Your crops will not be able to compete with them because these types of plants are aggressive. Weeds will compete with your plants in gaining water, nutrients and sunlight.

5. Protect the seedbed from disturbances

When you see the cotyledons come out of the ground, this means your seeds are growing as planned. Cotyledons are not yet true leaves. They serve as storage structures for energy and they are used in the first stage of the plant's development. You should not touch the plants when the cotyledons first appear. At this stage, the roots system is still developing. When the roots system is stable, the plant will grow its first set of leaves. These are the first true leaves of the plant. They are fully functional in converting raw materials into chemical energy usable by the plants.

In this part of the development, you need to protect the seedbed from the forces in its environment. If the soil becomes dry for too long, the seedling will die. If the heat of the sun is too strong, the cotyledon and the first set of leaves will shrivel and the plant will die. If you have chickens, they may eat the plants during these stages. Many factors may kill the plant at this stage.

To protect your seedlings, you need to make sure that these are located in an area where they cannot reach other animals in your area. You also need to protect them from direct noontime sun. They can withstand early morning and late afternoon sunlight, but noontime sun may be too strong. At this stage, the leaves do not have a lot of stored water. If exposed to strong sunlight for too long, they may become dehydrated and die.

Learn specific techniques of planting each seed

Not all seeds grow in the same way. Some seeds require special types of care before they can break out of their shell. You need to learn these special techniques for specific seeds. The instructions for planting are included in the seed's packaging.

Transplanting

Transplanting is the process of transferring the plants into the boxes that you prepared. In this process, it is important to make sure that the root system of the plants is not damaged in the transfer.

Seedlings are ready to transplant when they have several sets of true leaves. Water the seedbed before transplanting to loosen the soil. When transplanting them, you should lift them through their leaves. This will lessen the likelihood of damaging the stem and the roots.

You should then transfer them in their designated space in your square foot gardening box. After transplanting, you need to water the newly planted seedlings. The moist soil will encourage the roots to branch out and to hold on and absorb nutrients from its new soil.

Planting directly to the soil

In some cases, it may be prudent to plant some seeds directly to the square foot gardening boxes. Some types of seeds are just too fragile to be transplanted. In most cases, it will also be easier to space out small vegetables evenly in your boxes if you plant them directly into the box.

In planting small vegetables like radishes, you may fit up to 16 of them in one 1-square foot space. You can only plant this number in a space as small as this if you place the seeds strategically from day one. It will be more difficult to conserve space if you transplant grown plants into the box.

Positioning the plants

As mentioned earlier, a 4-square foot box has 16 1x1 foot squares. You can fit 16 small plants in these smaller squares. Small plants like carrots, radishes and white onions can be spaced evenly so that the four plants can fit on one side of the square.

To make 16 small carrots grow in a 1x1 foot square, divide that space into four by drawing a cross sign across the dirt. This will create four squares of the same size. Use your index and middle finger to poke two pairs of holes in this space. You can then drop the seeds in those holes. Do this step repeatedly until you have four holes in each of the squares.

Nine medium-sized plants can fit in the same space. Some examples of medium size plants are beets, bush beans and spinach. You can space them out evenly by drawing two evenly spaced lines inside the 1x1

Square Foot Gardening Guide

foot square. You should draw another pair of lines perpendicular to the first pair to make nine smaller boxes. You can then, plant the seedlings in the middle of the each of the nine boxes.

Only four large plants will fit the 1x1 foot space. Examples of large plants are lettuce, marigold and Swiss chard. Only one of the largest types of vegetables will fit in the same space. Examples of these types of plants are broccoli, cabbage and bell peppers.

Chapter 10 – Growing, Maintenance and Harvesting Tasks

After planting your fruits and vegetables, the next step is to sustain their growth. You can do this by defending them from threats, providing their needs and preventing them from occupying more than their designated space.

Here are some of the tasks that you need to do to keep your crops growing:

Watering

All plants require regular watering to grow. Most vegetables need to be watered daily especially in hot days. In cloudy days, the soil mix may remain wet even if you don't water them. This is due to the soil conditioner used such as peat moss or coir. You can add it to the soil to increase water retention.

When watering your square foot gardening boxes, be careful not to disturb too much of the top of the soil mixture. The mixture is lighter than regular soil because it has no rocks. When you first fill the box, you will notice that the mixture is still too loose. Watering it directly with a hose may displace the top part of the soil. When watering, use the sprinkler option in your hose head.

In the beginning, when you still have fewer boxes, you can water your plants using a handheld sprinkler. As you build more boxes and the task of watering becomes too troublesome, you can now use a hose system.

To automate the process, you may also use a sprinkler system. You can place the sprinkler head in the middle of all your boxes. This method however, is not efficient in using water.

A second option is to use a drip irrigation system. Gardeners, who arrange their plants on rows, use this system. However, you can also apply them in well-positioned square foot gardening boxes. Because you can position the water to exit right on the soil, this kind of system is more efficient.

Using an automated watering system saves you a lot of time in watering your plants. However, it also lessens your interactions with your plants. It is common for people to neglect their plants when they install these watering systems. You can avoid this by making it a habit to visit your garden at a specific time every day to check on your produce and your plants.

Mulching

Mulching is the process of adding compost on top of the soil. If you grow plants that last more than one planting season, you will need to mulch your soil to keep it nutrient-rich. Over time, some of the soil conditioning materials like the coir or peat moss decay. The soil's ability to hold water decreases when these materials completely decay. You should mulch once every year to keep the water retention properties of your soil high.

Weed watching

Even if you use prepared soil, some weed seeds may still reach your gardening box. The wind may bring them there or birds and other animals may carry them. Check your boxes for weeds regularly and remove them as soon as you see them. There is no need to use chemical products to remove weeds. Because we expect that there will only be a few of them over the course a planting season, you can just handpick them as soon as you see them.

Pest control

You will also need to do some pest control tasks when maintaining your square foot gardening boxes. As mentioned earlier, you need to keep the process organic when dealing with pests. The best way to deal with pests is to remove them manually when there are only few. You should remove them as soon as you see them. If you give them just a bit of time, then they may multiply beyond your ability to control them.

If you cannot handpick pets or if they become to numerous, you may need to turn to organic ways of killing large number of pests. The best method depends of the types of pests that you are dealing with.

Removal of unhealthy parts

You also need to track your plants for unhealthy parts. If you see that some leaves are damaged, for example, you may need remove them. Dead or wilting leaves may become the source of diseases. By removing them early, you can prevent decay to spread.

Harvesting tasks

This is the end goal for all your efforts. In traditional gardens, you harvest all the produce at the same time. This leads to an excess of supply at one time of the year. You can avoid this cycle when practicing square foot gardening.

Plan your whole activity so that you only get to harvest a small amount of a certain type of vegetables at one time. When certain plants are ready for harvesting in your garden, plan on how you can use them in your kitchen. If four of your lettuces are ready for harvest, you may plan to prepare different types of green salads for dinner in the next week.

To make sure that you do not plant more than you need, you should look forward into the harvesting date every time you plant something new. Before you plant 16 carrots, you need to plan the dishes where you will use all those carrots when you harvest them. You may also choose to give away some of them to your neighbors.

If you feel the urge to plant more, you may want to ask yourself if you will need more than 16 carrots at a time. If not, you should not plant any more. Instead of planting more of the same crop at the same time, you should reserve one 1x1-foot area for more carrots in the next month. This will ensure that you will have 16 more carrots in the following month.

You should always be aware of when your harvest dates will be. Before planting something, research how long it takes their fruits to mature. You should then plot the growth timeline on a calendar.

You may also try to synchronize the harvest time of plants that complement each other in the kitchen. If you are using carrots and potatoes together in a dish you like for example, you may choose to time your planting so that their harvest time are near each other.

Put plants that can be partially harvested together in one box. Leafy lettuce, for example, can be partially harvested and left to grow more leaves throughout the season. You may choose to let them grow in the same box with chards that can also be partially harvested. If you let them grow together, they will eventually make seeds that you can then harvest for the next planting season. If you already have enough seeds, you can just take one more harvest and plant another set of lettuce or chards.

You just continue this process until the winter. When the leaves in trees have completely fallen off, take one last harvest before winter comes. If you preserved some of your produce, you may use them throughout the winter.

When spring starts again, you can start replanting your preferred vegetables again.

Conclusion

Thank you again for purchasing this book!

I hope this book was able to help you to start your own organic square foot garden.

The next step is to make plans on how you can utilize the space you have efficiently. You can use the suggestions in this book to build your own square foot garden. In the beginning, you will make mistakes. However, as you gain experience in using this gardening system, you can avoid the same mistakes in the future.

My Free Gift To You!

Simon Hamilton

As a way of saying thank you for purchasing my book, I'd like to send you an exclusive gift that will help with organic composting.

I am giving you this FREE BONUS to thank you for being such an awesome reader and to make sure I give you all the value that I can in your mission to a better gardener!

To get your FREE gift, visit the URL below and follow the steps & I'll send it to your e-mail address right away.

www.gardenlovers.co

Finally, if you enjoyed this book, then I'd like to ask you for a favor, would you be kind enough to leave a review for this book on Amazon. It'd be greatly appreciated!

Thank you and good luck!

Made in the USA
Charleston, SC
04 September 2016